Lewis W. Hine

The Empire State Building

With an Introduction by
Freddy Langer

Prestel

Munich · London · New York

Front cover and spine: *Skyboy*
Back cover: *Looking down on two workers*

Page 1: *The Empire State Building*
Frontispiece: *The skyline of Manhattan from New Jersey*

The ever-soaring towers of mid-town Manhattan as seen looking across the
Hudson River from the New Jersey shore. William Van Alen's Chrysler
Building, finished in 1930, stands on the far left, its renowned stainless steel
pinnacle shining in the sun. On the far right looms Shreve, Lamb & Harmon's
Empire State Building of 1931, the quintessential symbol of the Empire State,
complete with a dirigible moored to its 200-foot mast.

From the Empire State Building Archive at the Avery Architectural
and Fine Arts Library, Columbia University in the City of New York;
back cover courtesy of the J. Paul Getty Museum, Los Angeles

Photography credits on p. 104

Library of Congress Cataloging-in-Publication Data

Hine, Lewis Wickes, 1874–1940.
   Lewis W. Hine : the Empire State Building / by Freddy Langer.
   p.   cm.
   ISBN 3-7913-1996-5 (alk. paper)
   1. Documentary photography--New York (State)--New York.
2. Construction workers--Pictorial works.   3. Hine, Lewis Wickes.
1874–1940. [1. Empire State Building (New York, N.Y.)--Design and
construction--Pictorial works.] I. Langer, Freddy, 1957- .
II. Title.   III. Title: Empire State Building.
TR820.5.H5634   1998
779'.969--dc21   98-34624
                                           CIP

© Prestel-Verlag 1998
Mandlstrasse 26, D-80802 Munich, Germany
Tel. +49 (89) 381709-0, Fax +49 (89) 381709-35
and 16 West 22nd Street, New York, NY 10010, USA
Tel. (212) 627-8199, Fax (212) 627-9866

Prestel books are available worldwide.
Please contact your nearest bookseller or write to either of the above
addresses for information concerning your local distributor.

Thanks to Susanne Baumann for her inspiration and
support on this project. J. T.

Translated from the German by Michele Schons
Edited by Claudine Weber-Hof

Designed by Daniela Petrini and Cilly Klotz
Lithography by Brend'amour, Munich
Cover paper and endpapers: Nettuno Blu Navy; Cartiere, Fedrigoni
Printed by Sellier, Freising
Bound by Oldenbourg, Kirchheim / Munich

Printed in Germany on acid-free paper
ISBN 3–7913–1996–5

Contents

Lewis W. Hine
Man and Work

The workers at the Empire State Building site made every conceivable effort to reassure the young photographer Lewis Wickes Hine, when, with a camera slung over his shoulder, he bravely followed them ladder by ladder up to the hundredth floor of the monolith under construction. He scaled heights that never before existed — or at least heights never before erected by the hands of men. Later, in his 1932 book entitled *Men at Work*, Hine would quote these "air treaders" as saying: "It isn't really as dangerous as it looks," and: "It's safer up here than it is down below," pointing down at the seething chaos of the streets of Manhattan, while balancing on narrow steel beams or allowing themselves to be lifted aloft on the giant iron hook of a derrick. Hine, who was described as being shy when it came to dealing with people, but who possessed a keen eye when it came to finding motifs, soon lost all fear of heights — and of the abyss below him. Hooked up to a safety line, he felt his way to the freely suspended ends of mooring masts to increase the dramatic effect of his photographs. As the project entered its final phase, he even swung from the rope tied to a derrick to get as far away from the building as was necessary to take pictures of the final rivet being secured at the tower's peak — with nothing under foot save "a sheer drop of nearly a quarter of a mile."

For six months in 1930 and 1931 Hine followed the construction of the world's tallest building. This was a miracle of the modern age — a new wonder being erected — and every moment of its creation, every vertical foot, every additional story, would be recorded. Unlike the wonders lost to ancient times — the Colossus of Rhodes, the Hanging Gardens of Babylon, or the Lighthouse of Alexandria, or enigmas archaeologists have been unable to determine, such as the construction of the Pyramids at Giza — the visual impact of this growing wonder would be documented in minute detail. Hine, however, was not overly concerned with the building itself and scarcely took notice of the beauty of its design. Rather than developing a distinct aesthetic sense for its elegant facade, its sleek, rocket-like form tapering towards the top, which appears to be closer to the sky than to the earth, Hine's interest was almost exclusively focused on the men occupied with building the skyscraper.

In the same straightforward manner that Hine photographed the building from street level, he took a picture of the plaque bearing the names of those men who had been presented with the

"Empire State Craftsmanship Award": they included George R. Adams, "painter and decorator," Vladimir Kozloff, "wrecker," and Thomas Walsh, "derrick man." The list of occupational titles must have reminded Hine of the index to his series of approximately 1,000 photographs of the Empire State Building under construction. Included were such titles as damp proofer, steam shovel operator, plasterer, glazier, sheet metal worker, and steam fitter's helper, as well as, naturally, cement mason, bricklayer, plumber, and carpenter and, in one instance simply "laborer" with the addition of a name, Guiseppe Rusciani, as though he represented the 2,500 to 4,000 laborers who worked at the construction site day in and day out. This, perhaps more than any other photograph taken by Hine, clearly demonstrates the photographer's attitude towards the workers. To him, they were all important — at least as important as the building itself.

In the short foreword to *Men at Work* — the only book Hine himself published on his works — Hine wrote: "Cities do not build themselves, machines cannot make machines, unless [at the] back of them all are the brains and toil of men. We call this the Machine Age. But the more machines we use the more do we need real men to make and direct them." With this volume of photographs he

established a memorial to these men, and a legacy to the high regard in which he held them.

Hine shows men in heroic poses, often stripped of their shirts, recalling the heroes depicted in Classical Greek statues. Some stand with steel cables in hand, pulling them taut, as though they were holding the globe in place. Others grapple with wrenches so large that they look as though they could set the clockwork of the earth's orbit in motion. Those wielding spirit levels look as though they were working to put life straight, while engineers using surveying equipment peer into the future and, with raised hands or a pointed finger, give instructions, directions, and leadership. Men holding welds, whose gas flames splinter into a thousand sparks, repelled by the iron they seek to master, create a veritable fireworks display as though rejoicing in work, the greatest of all celebrations. With these photographs Hine seems to be saying: those who can erect buildings such as this are capable of creating an entire world. This is where faith in technology and the ideal of a new, progressive urbanism crystallize into a single image. What failed in Babylon epochs earlier is finally brought to fruition in Manhattan.

Right to the end, Hine's admiration for the Empire State workers never diminished. He said he had become well acquainted with these men, who had educated themselves in the school of experience. Their muscles had been hardened through constant use, their eyes and nerves were fine-tuned, and they had the ability to work together, like players on a soccer field, and with the physical agility of acrobats. Never before had so much been conveyed by means of photography, least of all in architectural photography.

As long as skyscrapers have towered above the rooftops of American cities — that is, since the end of the nineteenth century — photographers have been fascinated by the new cityscape, in particular by the steeply ridged peaks and the deep, plunging ravines of the New York skyline. Though Chicago may have been home to the world's first skyscrapers, and may always have taken the lead in harboring the highest, most beautiful, most conspicuous skyscrapers — a term, after all, that was coined in the Windy City, first appearing in the *Chicago Tribune* on January 13, 1889 — it was of little long-term use to the city on Lake Michigan. The only buildings that were to become architectural icons in their own right towered over Manhattan, the center of American art and home to the preponderance of those photographers who employed their craft as an artistic endeavor.

These photographers' relationship to the high-flying architecture of the early twentieth century was marked by the same ambivalence with which the people of New York saw their city transformed into a megalopolis. On the one hand, America quite literally rose above itself; on the other hand, rapid growth cast ominous shadows at the foot of these architectural behemoths. The Pulitzer Building, completed in 1892, was the first building in Manhattan to tower above Trinity Church, which until then had

Alfred Stieglitz, *The Flatiron Building*, 1902–03

boasted the highest point in the city. Henceforth the cathedrals of commerce were to dominate the skyline. After the turn of the century, the Flatiron Building on Madison Square (1903), the Times Tower (1904), the Singer Building (1908), and the Woolworth Building (1913) followed. From a distance, New York began increasingly to resemble a fortified settlement, or a castle bristling with towers and battlements.

Photographers tried to scale the walls of the greatest city on earth, and at the time Alfred Stieglitz was undoubtedly the leading visionary amongst them. In his 291 Gallery and with his magazine *Camera Work*, he fostered the avant-garde of his day. At the same time he paved the way to the modern age with his own photographs: there, in the streets of New York, he would lie in wait for hours on end with his camera, heedless of snow storms, the rain, or the dark of night, in order to catch a glimpse of the city's strange and unparalleled charm. He spoke of capturing "picturesque bits"; however, in his photographs of train stations, harbors, coach stations, airplanes, and construction work on skyscrapers, he also found metaphors for the close of one era and the start of another. Above all else, his romantic consciousness ruled. In 1903 he photographed the Flatiron Building in the snow, silhouetted behind trees, as though it were part of an urban nature, an expression of harmony (see opposite page). In his 1910 photograph entitled *The City of Ambition* (see p. 11), the view across the East River to Manhattan is suffused with an almost religious quality, while the wisps issuing from the smokestacks recall the ritualistic burning of incense at a Catholic mass. Later, however, from 1930 onward, he recorded skyscrapers casting their shadows onto the urban landscape, enveloping it like some demonic force. It was not until this point that Stieglitz's photographs became critical commentaries.

Misgivings about modern cities such as these had already been formulated by Paul Strand — whom Stieglitz admired — in the photographs he took before World War I. Strand had a clear, accurate, if not utterly brutal view of reality, as well as a sound understanding of the lyrical qualities of the material world. Consequently, he was equally adept at wresting formally consummate, abstract motifs from facades and everyday objects by capturing a striking detail or by creating compositions with Cubist undertones. In so doing Strand conceived a new approach to beauty. He glorified technical devices, while leaving room for a critique of the world, as his most famous photograph, *Wall Street, New York* (see below), revealed: owing to the precipitous view of the sidewalk from above, the passersby appear small and insignificant, almost

Paul Strand,
*Wall Street,
New York,* 1916

insect-like, before four enormous, gaping windows. Stieglitz lost no time in publishing this photograph in *Camera Work*.

Berenice Abbott was another such brilliant observer of the world. She was drawn to photography by chance at the beginning of the 1920s in Paris, where Man Ray had employed her as his assistant. However, Man Ray's desire for artistic alienation came into conflict with Abbott's distanced way of seeing things. Later, she found both a mentor and a friend in Eugène Atget, who, at the turn of the century, had been endeavoring to capture scenes of old Paris on glass plates. In 1929, after Atget's death, Abbott returned to New

Berenice Abbott,
Wall Street:
Cliff and Ferry Streets

York with thousands of her mentor's photographs, intending to publish them. It was then she realized that the impending transformation of the city called for an approach similar to Atget's.

Those were the days, the final days, when two fundamentally different eras could be encountered in the city streets. One could observe horse-drawn vehicles, cable cars, and imposing limousines all at one glance. Housefronts reflecting the Victorian era could be seen juxtaposed with the unadorned facades of the modern age. It seemed merely a matter of months before the future would supersede the past, block for block. There was not much time left

for Abbott to document the present before its final and irrevocable break with all that had already come to be. She began to photograph, in part for an official commission, at the same time that Hine concluded his study of the Empire State Building. Nevertheless, her vision seemed to stem from a bygone era (see above, and pp. 13, 15). She seldom gave way to nostalgic longing. Instead, Abbott's motifs tell of the ambivalence with which the immense transformation at the beginning of the century was met. Her photographs in the book *Changing New York* represent a balancing act between horror and fascination.

With his contemporaries witnessing the threat of modern times, where did Hine derive his optimism, his confidence, thousands of feet above the city? How was he able to report in such an utterly compelling, inspired manner on the construction of the Empire State Building, when scenes from the streets must surely have taught him skepticism and doubt? On Thursday, October 24, 1929, the stock market crashed. It was the biggest financial debacle in history. In America, it was named "Black Thursday"; in Europe, where the news was made public the following day, it was "Black Friday" that all bemoaned. For four days the very foundations of the financial world shook, and on October 29 everything collapsed, including five thousand banks — nine million savings accounts vanished into thin air. The Great Depression ensued, with its thousands of insolvent businesses and millions of unemployed. Soup kitchens were set up in the cities, and lines of hungry people sometimes stretched beyond an entire city block. It took the economy nearly ten years to recover from the disaster.

Lewis Hine, however, seemed oblivious to it all. Resolutely, he followed an idea, for which he was willing to sacrifice reality. "I thought I had done my share of negative," he explained at the end of World War I, "I wanted to do something positive. So I said to myself, 'Why not do the worker at work?'" At a time when the worker was "as underprivileged as the kid in the mill," Hine felt "an urgent need for intelligent interpretation of the world's workers, not only for people of today, but for future ages." He had seen enough of misery.

Indeed, Hine began his work as a photographer by documenting the dark side of the great American dream. He did not consider himself an artist who wrestled with aesthetic matters; nor did he feel the compulsion to dissect, to improve, or to interpret the world. In advertisements for his small business — a studio and a handful of employees — he used the term "social photography." In essays and discussions, he referred to himself as a "concerned photographer." Lewis Hine was a reformer with a camera, convinced that hardship was the result of neither incompetence nor a lack of assiduity, and that poverty did not necessarily presuppose moral dubiousness. He ascribed prejudices to a lack of enlightenment, which he tried to counteract by sensitizing the public to the social injustices of the economic system. During the industrial reconstruction period he revealed the other side of the upswing: poverty, exploitation, violence, and corruption. He found inhumane conditions all around him, and, through his pictures, brought them over the factory walls, beyond the borders of the ghettos, and into the public consciousness, driven by the hope that things might change, at least in the long run.

Berenice Abbott,
Wall Street:
South and DePeyster Streets

Hine was himself intimately acquainted with the dark side of life, although his childhood was a happy one. He was born on September 26, 1874, in Oshkosh, Wisconsin, where his parents owned a coffee shop and as a child he enjoyed a sheltered upbringing. In 1892, the year he graduated from high school, everything changed. His father was killed in an accident, and for many years thereafter he was compelled to take on numerous odd jobs in factories, stores, and banks, where, in his own words, he was promoted to the rank of "supervising sweeper" — experiences that would leave their mark on him his entire life. Nonetheless, he managed to secure a college education by taking a correspondence degree course and by attending classes at the University of Chicago. There he studied under John Dewey and Ella Flagg Young, two of the nation's most prominent liberal educators. It was the principal of the State Nominal School in Oshkosh, Frank A. Manny, himself a disciple of progressive teaching principles, who met Hine in the bank one day and convinced him to pursue higher education. Manny, although only a few years older than Hine, was to become his mentor and was perhaps even a father figure for him. When Manny was appointed superintendent of the Ethical Culture School in New York in 1901, he took Hine with him as a teacher.

It was also at Manny's suggestion that Hine began to take photographs, initially of the school, but also of subjects beyond its walls. Manny regarded photography as an educational tool that effectively conveyed information. Often confronted in the classroom with prejudices against foreigners, he suggested that Hine photograph the immigrants arriving on Ellis Island so that the students "may have the same regard for contemporary immigrants as they have for the pilgrims who landed at Plymouth Rock."

Hine worked with a plate-back camera on a wobbly tripod, lit lycopodium powder in a bowl for a flash, and had to convince people, whose language he did not speak, to pose for his pictures. Despite the unfavorable circumstances, he produced deeply moving photographs: families behind bars, men sitting on suitcases, women bearing heavy loads on their heads, mothers with children in their arms, and children holding hands with their younger siblings. They all displayed similar facial expressions: a mixture of uncertainty, curiosity, displeasure, apprehensiveness, and anxiety. However, in none of his pictures is either a trace of courage or a hint of resignation discernible. Hine sought a type of zero sum, a balance of the most extreme emotions, the turning point in a person's life — the moment when the old life was over and the new one had not yet begun. It was 1905, and everything would change for Hine, too, after he had taken these pictures.

Three years later Hine left the Ethical Cultural School to devote himself exclusively to socially-committed photography. In the meantime he had earned a master's degree in sociology at Columbia University. He had also become acquainted with Arthur and

Paul Underwood Kellogg, Hine's lifelong collaborator and champion

Paul Kellogg, both editors at the newly founded weekly *Charities and the Commons*, a social welfare magazine that was to be renamed *The Survey* and, later, the *Survey Graphic*. Hine provided them with photo essays, and, in addition to teaching, the photographer also began to take pictures for the National Child Labor Committee (NCLC), which fought for legislation prohibiting child labor. The committee employed Hine, who would continue to work for them for the next ten years, and whose camera became their weapon against those who claimed that "such conditions did not exist." Collecting evidence became an obsession. Hine traveled tens of thousands of miles in the East, the Midwest, and the South, producing over 1,000 photographs. He even spoke of his vocation as "detective work."

Hine's photographs appeared in magazines and portfolios, were on display in traveling exhibitions and slide shows, and were used to illustrate pamphlets. For many it was an utterly new world that Hine presented to them: the world of slums and back allies, cramped quarters with no running water or electricity, sparcely furnished with pieces taken from the garbage. Scenes of exploitation were also presented, such as an entire family gathered together around a table, cracking nuts or weaving handmade flowers for less than a dollar a day.

But the most harrowing pictures are those of children working. "There is work that profits the children, and there is work that brings profit only to the employers," he once wrote in the *Child Labor Bulletin*. "The object of employing children is not to train them, but to get high profits from their work." It was a waste of human life. "Human junk" was thus produced, Hine said on more than one occasion.

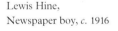

Lewis Hine,
Newspaper boy, *c.* 1916

With ever-new pretexts he managed to smuggle himself past factory guards. According to legend, he sometimes claimed to be a Bible salesman. Other times he professed to have been commissioned to photograph the plant's machinery. In reality, however, he took photographs of young girls positioned between the giant machines of textile factories or young boys in dark mineshafts. Hine visited canneries, tobacco manufacturers, glassworks, and spinning mills. He photographed children rolling cigarettes and delivering newspapers (see p. 17). He found the same images everywhere: broken bodies, vacant stares, and children wearing rags instead of clothes. At this point in time he, the outraged critic, was neither interested in subtle observation nor in discreet innuendo. He strove for effects, bold effects. In describing the thrust of his work Hine was quoted as saying: "Whether it be a painting or a photograph, the picture is a symbol that brings one immediately into close touch with reality. In fact, it is often more effective than reality would have been, because, in the picture, the non-essential and conflicting interests have been eliminated." The authenticity of his work and his photographs was underscored by his attempts to speak at length to each and every child, to note down their names, ages, heights, situations at home, jobs, how long they had been employed, whether they were ill, and whether they attended school.

Through its active campaign and, no doubt, owing to Hine's unsettling photographs, the National Child Labor Committee celebrated the successful passing of social legislation in 1916. Congress reacted and President Woodrow Wilson signed an act that prohibited child labor. Proponents of the Progressive Movement were naturally that much more disappointed when, two years later, the Supreme Court declared the law unconstitutional. Some twenty years would pass before Franklin D. Roosevelt would sign the Labor Standards Act of 1938.

That Lewis Hine had a falling out with the National Child Labor Committee in 1918 had nothing to do with the legislative setback, but instead with a difference of opinion he had with the organization regarding his responsibilities — and with a disagreement over his salary. After Hine resigned, he sought a new theme and found new manifestations of misery — this time in Europe, where, in November of the same year, he accompanied the so-called "Special Survey" division of the American Red Cross, which had set out to document "the human costs of war." For some six months Hine traveled in Italy, Serbia, and Greece, and later in Belgium and France. It was during these trips, despite the human tragedy in the ravaged cities and countryside, that he first perceived expressions of honor, strength, and courage in people's faces. Even children leaning on crutches looked bravely into his camera. This experience would have a considerable effect on his future work in the United States, and from this point on advertisements of his read: "Lewis W. Hine, Interpretive Photography."

"There were two things I wanted to do. I wanted to show the things that had to be corrected. I wanted to show the things that had to be appreciated," later Hine said in explaining the break in his work. Suddenly Hine celebrated workers, regarding them as the true heroes of modern society. He no longer saw them as a cog in a machine, but instead as the underpinning element of the enormous driving force called America. To show "that the worker is not a lower form of life" became his new creed. With his *Work Portraits* he depicted "industry from a human angle" — to the point that his pictures of laborers fell just short of Social Realism.

"As I see it, the great problem of industry is to go a step beyond merely having the employer and employee get along. The employee must be induced to feel a pride in his work," wrote Hine in his article 'He Who Interprets Big Labor,' published in the periodical *The Mentor* in September 1926.

> *I try to do with the camera what the writer does with words. People can be stirred to a realization of the values of life by writing. Unfortunately many persons don't comprehend good writing. On the other hand, a picture makes its appeal to everyone. Put into the picture an idea and, if properly used, it may be transferred to the brain of the worker. … Interpretive photography … will do that, I know, for it has been done. The great problem, of course, is to link the employer and employees in this method of education so that each sees the value in it. The employer must think of it as genuine, not paternalistic; the employee must think of it as a sincere treatment of him and his work, not flattery.*

With this said, Hine himself became one of the greatest flatterers of all. He increasingly presented railroad men, mechanical engineers, and even miners as the conductors of a complex system. Craftsmen of all kinds, though not industrial workers, are shown energetically screwing bolts, hammering nails, and opening valves. Their drills, milling cutters, hammers, and wrenches appear to be extensions of their bodies. "Productive" energy became one of Hine's key terms. And nowhere did it manifest itself more clearly than in these photographs. Men and work became synonymous. To Hine *Men at Work* was not merely the title of a book; for him it became an agenda. He positively extolled the "courage, skill, daring and imagination" of these workers. Introducing the iconic photographs presented in his book is an excerpt from William James' essay entitled 'The Moral Equivalent of War': "Not in clanging fights and desperate marches only is heroism to be looked for, but on every bridge and building that is going up today, on freight trains, on vessels and lumber-rafts, in mines, among firemen and policemen, the demand for courage is incessant and the supply never fails. These are our soldiers, our sustainers, the very parents of our life."

Such glorification of the working class found heightened expression in Hine's photographs of the Empire State Building under

construction. It was the apotheosis. "I have always avoided dare-devil exploits and do not consider these experiences as going quite that far — but they have given me a new zest," wrote the photo-grapher after he had completed the series, "and perhaps a different note in my interpretation of Industry."

It was as though, through industrial photography, he wished to contribute to the formation of the growing nation's identity. Just as the pioneers had once explored the vast expanse of the country, and in doing so, founded a new world, so, too, would a new person emerge from the tasks of industrialization — and a new civilization from their achievements. In retrospect one might think that Hine intended to present a great social novel in pictures through his oeuvre, his photographic *condition humaine* — with an unmistak-ably happy end: first the immigrants who possess nothing more than the clothes on their bodies and a few belongings in their bags and suitcases. Then the inhumane, unsanitary conditions in which they lived in dark apartments and dirty courtyards. And, finally, their excellent work performance: the new, dazzling world that they created for themselves, and for humanity. Hine's pictures were metaphors for the birth of a global economic power. Nevertheless, reality demanded an epilogue.

Hine, of course, could not keep his eyes closed indefinitely to the country's economic crisis. The fact that he, once the tireless defender of workers' rights, took on an increasing number of jobs for large corporations, left him feeling unsettled. Even his photographs of the Empire State Building were commissioned by the Empire State Corporation and were intended for use as advertising material. It thus seems telling that Hine, who indefatigably wrote letters and who frequently published articles, only rarely made reference to his work on the Empire State Building. His letter to Florence Kellogg, art editor at the *Survey Graphic*, in January 1931, ended with the cryptic comment: "Many thanks for all your sympathy, patience and encouragement. Even skyscrapers have their basements and skyscraping has its rebounds & depressions."

As late as 1933, Hine still insisted "that the human spirit is the big thing after all." The publication of his book the previous year earned him numerous commissions — even from private industry, such as the weaving mill Shelton Looms, whose president, Sidney Blumenthal, was considered to be one of the most progressive leaders in industry management. The government's Work Progress Administration hired Hine to document the construction of their boldest project, set in an impoverished region: the Tennessee Valley

Lewis Hine,
Manhattan skyline with
Empire State Building

Authority of Clinch Valley, which included a dam, a power station, artificial irrigation plants, as well as electricity and water supplies. However, his desire to work for the Farm Security Administration — for which such prominent photographers as Walker Evans, Dorothea Lange, Arthur Rothstein, and Russell Lee traveled through the American South and Midwest to capture the effects of the Depression on farmers — remained unfulfilled, despite his persistent efforts to secure a commission. His reputation as a contrary person and reports from previous employers, such as "Is true artist type. Requires handling as such," closed doors for him. Instead, in 1936 he was appointed chief photographer of the Works Progress Administration's National Research Project on Reemployment Opportunities and Recent Changes in Industrial Techniques, which was responsible for recording the success of Roosevelt's New Deal politics — an economic and socio-political reform program with which the government intended to counteract the economic crisis.

This is where Hine's emphatic depiction of the worker assumed its final form. In his photographs of automated production lines it becomes clear that skill and craftsmanship were no longer in demand. Here, before huge, intimidating machines, the relationship was reversed: the human being seemed to have become a slave to the machine. This revelation could have been a new, important theme for the photographer, but he was running low on strength, commissions, and money.

Hine's early photographs were rediscovered in the late 1930s and were celebrated once again. Beaumont Newhall, former curator of photography at the Museum of Modern Art in New York, gave the photographer a place in the photographic Hall of Fame when he wrote in the *Magazine of Art* in 1938, "These photographs were taken primarily as records. They are direct and simple. The presence in them of an emotional quality raises them to works of art." An exhibition of Hine's photographs followed shortly thereafter at the Riverside Museum in New York. However, fate had it in for him. He scarcely received any more commissions, and after several years of impoverishment, in 1939, he lost his wife to illness. A little later, he lost his house. He died on November 4, 1940, at the age of sixty-six — himself a hardship case.

Freddy Langer

Material quoted in the essay is from the following sources:

Doherty, Jonathan L., ed. *Women at Work: 153 Photographs by Lewis W. Hine.* New York: Dover Publications, 1981.
Gutman, Judith Mara. *Lewis W. Hine: 1874–1940.* New York: Grossman Publishers, 1974.
Hine, Lewis W. *Men at Work: Photographic Studies of Modern Men and Machines.* New York: Dover Publications, 1977 (originally published by the Macmillan Company, New York, 1932).
Kaplan, Daile, ed. *Photo Story: Selected Letters and Photographs of Lewis W. Hine.* Washington, D.C.: Smithsonian Institution Press, 1992.
Kemp, John R., ed. *Lewis Hine: Photographs of Child Labor in the New South.* Jackson: University Press of Mississippi, 1986.

PLATES

*The Men Who
Built the Empire
State Building*

Checking to see if the building is "true"

Honored with an award for craftsmanship

Drilling the foundations

Unloading steel

The heater gets the bolts red hot
and tosses them to the riveters

Portrait of an unidentified construction worker

An early phase of construction

Constantly checking progress:
an engineer with a theodolite

35

Workers guiding a hoisting cable

One of the many derrick operators

Portrait of an unidentified construction worker

Turning and directing a derrick

Synchronized efforts to build the Empire State

The derricks that built the Empire State

Team work

A derrick man

Moving girders into place

The "best bricklayer in New York" hard at work

Stonemasons at work

Inspecting the progress from a derrick lift

Welder

Tightening the bolts

Two workers securing a rivet

No fear of heights

The riveter, bucker-up, and catcher secure the girders

Moving on up

No time to admire the view

Workmen high above the Chrysler Building

Bolting a corner of the tower together almost 100 stories up

At work on a corner of the tower

Portrait of an unidentified construction worker

Working on the steel structure of the mooring mast

No rules, no restrictions, no safety precautions

Taking a break high above Manhattan

Steelwork, mooring mast

A cigarette and a view: a worker taking a break

Two workers inspecting the steel structure

A hoister guiding steel girders

Putting girders into place

Rivet gang at work:
The catcher (left) picks the red-hot bolt out of the air with his
tin scoop; the bucker-up (middle) holds the rivet in place while
the riveter (right) drives home the bolt with his pneumatic gun

Looking down on two workers

Portrait of an unidentified construction worker

Preparing to hoist a girder

Connectors aloft

A connector waiting for a girder

Maneuvering the girder

Connectors bolt the girder into place

The view onto Lower Manhattan
from the Empire State Building

Portrait of an unidentified worker holding a bucket

Visiting inspector

Repetition of the same specialized task allows the building to grow
up and over Manhattan at the rate of 4 ½ stories per week

Connectors placing a girder

Skyboy

Stunning views from the skeletal structure

Steelworker on the 86th floor

A connector on the move

Derricks

Constructing the frame of the observatory tower

Men at the top of a derrick

Starting to "jump the derrick"

The skyline of Manhattan from New Jersey

The McClain Brothers

The Empire State Building after completion

APPENDIX

The Empire State Building in Brief

1799: The City of New York sells a virgin tract (now bounded by Broadway and Sixth Avenue on the West, Madison Avenue on the East, 33rd Street on the South, and 36th Street on the North) to John Thompson, a farmer, for $2,600.

1825: Charles Lawton buys the farm from Thompson for $10,000.

1827: William B. Astor, the second son of John Jacob Astor, purchases the farm for $20,500 as an investment property.

1859: John Jacob Astor Jr. builds a mansion on the northwest corner of 33rd Street and Fifth Avenue.

1862: William B. Jacob, John Jacob Jr.'s older brother, builds his mansion next door, on the southwest corner of 34th Street and Fifth Avenue.

1893: William Waldorf Astor, son of John Jacob Astor Jr., tears the mansion down and erects the Waldorf Hotel on the corner of Fifth Avenue and 33rd Street.

1897: Mrs. William Backhouse Astor, John Jacob Jr.'s aunt, allows her mansion at 34th Street and Fifth Avenue to be razed and the Astoria Hotel is erected on the site. The new structure becomes known as the Waldorf-Astoria Hotel.

1928: The Waldorf-Astoria Hotel is sold to Bethlehem Engineering Corporation for an estimated $20 million. The architectural firm of Shreve and Lamb is put on retainer for the Empire State project. Harmon becomes Shreve and Lamb's partner during the final designs for the Empire State Building.

1929: John Jacob Raskob (creator of General Motors), Coleman du Pont (president of E.I. Du Pont de Nemours), Louis G. Kaufman, and Ellis P. Earl form Empire State, Inc. and name Alfred E. Smith, former Governor of New York and Presidential candidate, to head the corporation.

1930: Construction of the Empire State Building begins in January, and proceeds at a rapid rate.

1931: On May 1 President Herbert Hoover officially opens the Empire State Building, switching on its lights with the press of a button.

1951: The Empire State Building is sold by the John J. Raskob estate for $34 million to a group headed by Roger I. Stevens; the Prudential Insurance Company of America buys the Empire State for $17 million and enters into a long-term ground lease with the owners.

1954: A Chicago group headed by Col. Henry J. Crown buys the Empire State for $51.5 million.

1961: On December 27, Empire State Building Associates, an investment syndicate created by Lawrence A. Wien, purchases a 114-year master leasehold of the land and Building for $36 million; at the same time, the Prudential Insurance Company of America buys the Building for $29 million. Col. Crown, as seller, receives the total of $65 million, at that time, the highest price ever paid for a New York City property. Principals in the closing include Lawrence A. Wien and Peter L. Malkin, Esq., general partners of Empire State Building Associates; Col. Henry Crown, Chairman and principal stockholder of Empire State Building Corporation; Harry B. Helmsley, principal broker in the transaction; and Louis B. Menagh, president of Prudential Insurance Company.

The Empire State Building Company operates the Empire State Building as the sublease of Empire State Building Associates, a partnership led by Peter L. Malkin and represented by Wien & Malkin, LLP.

Helmsley-Spear, Inc., is the managing agent for the Empire State Building. In the year 2076, the master lease will expire and control of the property will pass to NS 1999, which purchased the property in 1993.

Basic Facts and Vital Statistics

Architects: Shreve, Lamb & Harmon Associates

Contractor: Starrett Brothers and Ekin

Excavation: Begun on January 22, 1930

Construction: Commenced March 17, 1930. The framework rose at a rate of 4½ stories per week.

Cornerstone: Original laid by Alfred E. Smith on September 17, 1930. The 50th anniversary edition was installed in May, 1981.

Masonry: Completed on November 13, 1930.

Total time: Completed ahead of schedule. One year and 45 days including Sundays and holidays. Opened May 1, 1931

Man hours: 7,000,000

Cost: $40,948,900 (including land)

Building costs: $24,718,000 (the onset of the Depression halved the anticipated cost of the building)

Area of site: 79,288 square feet (7,366 square meters) or about two acres. East to West, 424 feet (129 meters), North to South, 187 feet (56.9 meters)

Foundation: 55 feet (16.7 meters below ground)

Basement: 35 feet (10.6 meters below ground)

Lobby: 47 feet (14.3 meters) above sea level

Total height: 1,454 feet (1,453 feet, 8⁹⁄₁₆th inches) or 443.2 meters to top of lightning rod.

To 86th floor observatory: 1,050 feet (320 meters)

102nd floor to tip: 203 feet (61.8 meters)

Antenna height: 18 feet (5.5 meters)

Floors: 102

Steps: 1,860 from street level to 102nd floor

Volume: 37 million cubic feet

Weight: 365,000 tons

Plan: The building's base reaches five floors above the street, the entrance is four floors high, and lobby is three floors high. Beginning with the 60-foot setback on the fifth floor, the building rises sheer to the 86th floor.

Air conditioning: Provided by 8,100 connected tons of refrigeration equipment of 10,111 ton availability. The original air conditioning was installed in 1950, and was upgraded in 1984 and 1994.

Water: 70 miles of pipe provide water from the pump room in the lower level to tanks throughout the building, with the uppermost on the 101th floor. The water system must satisfy an average daily demand of 26,500 cubic feet (750 cubic meters) with 74,000 gallons (336,400 liters) on reserve at all times.

Electricity: The 40 million kilowatt hours needed by building and tenants each year flow through 2,500,000 feet (762,000 meters) of electrical wire.

Fire safety: A state of the art electronic fire control and alarm system stands guard over the building. A special water system feeds 400 firehose connections, and the fire pump system has a total capacity of 3,250 gallons per minute, with 13 external fire department connections.

Telephone cable: 1,060 air miles of telephone cable serve tenants.

Waste: 100 tons of trash and waste are removed from the building each month.

Staff: About 300 people staff the building, including a maintenance crew of more than 150 persons.

Elevators: 73 (including 6 freight elevators) serve floors from the Lower Lobby to the 102nd floor. 8 escalators serve the Concourse Level and 2nd floor. Passenger elevators are all computer controlled and travel up to speeds of 1,200 feet (366 meters) per minute.

One of the hundreds of site workers

Amenities and Attractions

Observatories

Location: 86th and 102nd floors. The 86th floor observatory features a heated, glassed-in area ringed by an outdoor terrace. There high-power binoculars offer spectacular vistas. The 102nd floor observatory is fully enclosed.

Hours: 9:30 a.m. to midnight, daily. The last tickets are sold at 11:30 p.m.

Admission: Adults: $6.00; Children ages 6–11 years, Senior Citizens, & Military: $3.00; Children under 6, and Military in uniform are given complimentary admission. (Group rates are available). Tickets may be purchased at the observatory ticket office on the concourse, one level below the ground floor.

Visitors: Over 3.5 million people visit the observatories each year, with as many as 30,000 on weekends. Since the opening of the building in 1931, there have been more than 117,000,000 visitors, the 50 millionth visited in 1965, the 110 millionth in 1989.

Views: As they say, "On a clear day, you can see forever." And the Observatory ticket office posts a sign telling just how far forever is. On the clearest of days, visibility is 80 miles, taking in five states — New York, New Jersey, Pennsylvania, Connecticut, and Massachusetts. Its situation in midtown Manhattan affords a 360° unobstructed sighting of the cityscape, bridges and environs. You can see all New York in one stop. By day, the view is a lesson in geography and meteorology. By night, it's a spill of jewels on black velvet.

Shops and Services

Banks, doctors, dentists, a post office, card shop, shoe repair shop, clothing stores, jewelers, coffee shops, restaurants, newsstands, Federal Express, a photography store, drug store, and many others.

Tower Lights – 1931 to the Present Day

1932: The first light to shine atop the Empire State Building in November, was a searchlight beacon which indicated to people for 50 miles around that Franklin D. Roosevelt had been elected president.

1956: Four revolving synchronized beacons, the "Freedom Lights", were installed. The "Freedom Lights," four beacons each five feet in diameter

Connectors securing
a girder into place

and weighing one ton, were installed 1,095 feet (333.8 meters) above the streets to symbolize not only a welcome to this country but also the unlimited opportunities of America and the hopes and prayers of the American people for peace.

1964: The top 30 floors of the building were illuminated by a new series of floodlights in April, transforming the Empire State Building into a night-time landmark at the beginning of the New York World's Fair.

1976: Colored lighting was first introduced by Douglas Leigh. The tower was lit in red, white and blue in celebration of the American Bicentennial.

1977: A new lighting system, permitting a wider range of colors, was inaugurated on October 12, when blue and white lights flashed to announce that the Yankees baseball team had won the World Series.

The installation of 204 fixtures, utilizing metal halide lamps, plus 310 fluorescent lamps, light the top 30 floors of the building from the 72nd floor to the base of the television antenna.

Plastic gels are fitted manually over the metal halide lamps, or floodlights, and colored plastic sleeves are fitted over the fluorescent tubes in a variety of color combinations to honor national holidays and events of interest to New Yorkers.

The lamps create a candle power of 1,000 watts each. This system uses less energy than the original system, thus complying with energy conservation programs.

1984: Automation of fluorescent color-changing apparatus in the uppermost mooring mast. Designed by Douglas Leigh with Charles Guigno, Empire State Building director of operations, 880 vertical 75-watt fluorescent tubes in the mast and 220 horizontal fluorescents at the base of the mast can now be changed at the flick of a switch. Installed in each face of the mast are four vertical banks of 11 8-foot panels positioned one on top of another. Each of the 176 panels contains 5 tubes and each tube is a different color — red, green, blue, yellow, and white. Additionally, at the base of the mast, there are 44 newly installed panels of horizontal fluorescents, also containing five colored tubes each, totaling 220 tubes. A new ring of 32 high-pressure sodium vapor lights, 70 watts each, above the 102nd floor, was installed to create a golden "halo" effect around the top of the mast from dusk to dawn.

Taking the strain

Colors for Celebrated Days and Events (listed from base to top)

Red, black, and green: Dr. Martin Luther King Jr., Day

Green: St. Patrick's Day, Rainforest Awareness

Red, white, and blue: Presidents' Day, Armed Forces Day, Memorial Day,
    Flag Day, Independence Day, Labor Day, Veterans' Day

Red: St. Valentine's Day, Fire Prevention Week

Yellow, white: Spring, Easter Week

Blue, white, blue: Israel Independence Day

Blue: Police Memorial Day

Red, yellow, green: Portugal Day

Lavender, white: Stonewall Anniversary / Gay Pride

Yellow: POW / MIA Recognition

Red, white: Pulaski Day

Red, white, green: Columbus Day

Blue, white: Greek Independence Day, United Nations Day

Red, yellow: Autumn (Halloween to Thanksgiving)

Black, yellow, red: German Reunification Day

Purple, white: Alzheimer's Awareness

Pink, white: "Race For The Cure" — Breast Cancer

Green, white, orange: India Independence Day

Red, green: Holiday Season

Dark, no lights: "Day Without Art / Night Without Lights" — Aids Awareness

Other than the above listed special occasions, and others such as the New York
    Yankees or New York Mets baseball teams winning the pennant and/or
    World Series, the homecoming of troops from Operation Desert Storm,
    and other one time events, white lighting is used.

Other Facts

Wonders of the World:

Since June, 1963, the 34th Street lobby has housed eight massive illuminated
    color panels by artists Roy Sparkia and his wife Renee Nernerov who inter-
    preted the Seven Wonders of the Ancient World — and the Eighth Wonder
    of the modern world, the Empire State Building.

These unique artworks provide three-dimensional softly lit pictures of:

Great Cheops Pyramids (481 feet, or 146 meters high)

Hanging Gardens of Babylon (30 feet, or 9 meters high)

Statue of Zeus (40 feet, or 12 meters high)

Temple of Diana (over 50 feet, or 15 meters high)

Lighthouse of Pharos, Alexandria (600 feet, or 183 meters high)

Colossus of Rhodes (160 feet, or 49 meters high)

Tomb of King Mausolus

The Empire State Building (1,454 feet, or 443 meters high)

Mooring mast: A dirigible mast, now the base of the TV tower, was part of the
    original construction of the Building. One attempt to moor a privately
    owned blimp was successful for three minutes. But during a second at-
    tempt, in September 1931, a Navy blimp was almost upended and nearly
    swept away celebrities attending the historic affair, while the water ballast
    drenched pedestrians several blocks away. The mooring mast idea was ulti-
    mately abandoned.

Bomber crash: On July 28, 1945, an Army Air Force B-25 crashed into the
    Building between the 79th and 80th floors. Fourteen people died. Damage
    to the Building was $1 million but the structural integrity of the Building
    was not effected.

Dominating the intersection at
34th Street and 5th Avenue

Points of Interest:

The display on the second floor features special exhibits highlighting the flavor of New York, including museums, cultural institutions and tourist attractions.

Fifth Avenue gallery windows: The Fifth Avenue lobby features six display windows which exhibit art and memorabilia from New York City's myriad museums, galleries and artists. The exhibits change several times a year.

Air race checkpoint: In May, 1969, the Building was one of the two checkpoints in the transatlantic air race commemorating the 50th anniversary of the first transatlantic flight by two British pilots.

Datum point: The Empire State Building is located at: Latitude 40° 44' 553.977" North and Longitude 73° 59' 10.812 West

VIP photos: The world's famous have come to admire the unmatched view from the Empire State Building's observatories. Photos of some of them are on display in the observatory ticket office on Concourse Level. Visitors have included heads of state from almost every country in the world, film stars (including Lassie, the television show dog star), U.S. political figures and men and women of every accomplishment.

Building sway: The Empire State Building does not sway … it gives. With a wind of 110 miles an hour, the Building gives 1.48 inches (3.76 cm). Movement off center is never greater than one quarter inch, thus measurable movement is only one half inch, one quarter inch on either side.

Bird migrations: During the spring and fall bird migrations season, the lights that illuminate the Building tower are turned off on foggy nights so it will not confuse the birds and invite them to fly into the Building.

Landmark status: On May 18, 1981, the Building (exterior and lobby) was declared a Landmark by the New York City Landmarks Preservation Commission. On December 20, 1982, the Building was listed on the State and National Register of Historic Places. On October 23, 1986, it was recognized as a National Historic Landmark by the National Parks Services, U.S. Department of the Interior, and garnered a commemorative plaque.

King Kong: On April 7, 1983, King Kong returned to the Empire State Building to celebrate his 50th anniversary. Fans the world over cheered his triumphant ascent. The 84-foot, 3,000-pound inflatable Kong was created by Robert Vicino, president of Robert Keith & Co., Inc., engineered by consultants Geiger Berger Associates, PC, and rigged by Lime Waterproofing, Inc. King Kong and the Empire State Building have been partners since 1933, when the landmark film was released.

Kissing: Static electricity buildup is so mammoth on top of the Building that, under the right conditions, if you put your hand through the observatory fence, St. Elmo's Fire will stream from your fingertips. Lovers who kiss atop the Empire State may find their lips crackling with electric sparks.

Neighbors: The Building is at the heart of a shopping district which includes Macy's, Herald Center, Lord & Taylor, and Manhattan Mall. It's a short stroll from Times Square, Madison Square Garden, Madison Square Park, the Flatiron Building, the New York Public Library, Bryant Park, the Little Church Around the Corner, the General Post Office Building, and the Jacob Javits Convention Center.

Movies in which the Empire State Building has Appeared:

Across the Sea of Time
An Affair To Remember
Annie Hall
Any Wednesday
April Fools
Ask Any Girl
Auntie Maine
Bachelor Apartment
Ball of Fire
Bell Book and Candle
Best of Everything
Big City
Big City Blues
Blackboard Jungle
Bon Voyage
Broadway Melody
Butcher's Wife
Champion
Charlie Chan of Broadway
Come to the Stable
Coogan's Bluff
Daddy Long Legs
Detective Story
Easter Parade
Edge of the City
FBI Story
Fine Madness
Finian's Rainbow
Fitzwilly
Footlight Serenade
For Pete's Sake
French Connection I

French Line
Funny Face
Funny Girl
Garment Jungle
Girl 6
Godzilla
Guys & Dolls
Hackers
Hatful of Rain
How to Succeed in Business
I Take This Woman
It's Always Fair Weather
Ivory Ape
King Kong
King of the Gypsies
Klute
Kramer vs. Kramer
Last Action Hero
Law & Disorder
Love Affair
Love With a Proper Stranger
Lullaby of Broadway
Madigan
Man in Gray Flannel Suit
Manhattan
Manhattan Melodrama
Money Train
Moon is Blue
My Man Godfrey
*   (remake)*
My Sister Eileen
New York Confidential

New York, New York
New York Stories
New York Town
North by Northwest
Nothing Sacred
On the Town
On the Waterfront
Pawnbroker
President's Analyst
Prisoner of Second Avenue
Rock Around the Clock
Saboteur
Safety First
Saint in New York
Serpico
Seven Ups
Shaft
Sky's the Limit
Slaughter on Tenth Avenue
Sleepless in Seattle
So This is New York
Stand Up and Cheer
Street Scene
Sunday in New York
Superman II
Sweet Charity
Taxi Driver
When Harry Met Sally
Who Done It
World Flesh & Devil
World of Henry Orient
You Gotta Stay Happy

Photographic Credits

All photographs by Lewis W. Hine, various formats and media, 1930–31, courtesy of: The Empire State Building Archive at the Avery Architectural and Fine Arts Library, Columbia University in the City of New York, with the exception of the following: p. 6, courtesy George Eastman House; p. 10 (photogravure, 17 × 8.3 cm), and p. 11 (photogravure, 33.9 × 26 cm), © Estate of Georgia O'Keeffe, courtesy of the J. Paul Getty Museum, Los Angeles; p. 13 (#49, 40.140.38), p. 14 (#48, 40.140.142), p. 15 (#52, 40.140.233), © Museum of the City of New York; p. 16, courtesy of the Social Welfare History Archives, University of Minnesota; p. 17, by Lewis W. Hine, courtesy of the Freddy Langer Collection, Frankfurt am Main; p. 18 (gelatin silver, 24.4 × 19.4 cm), p. 71 and back cover (gelatin silver, 24.1 × 19.2 cm), p. 92 (gelatin silver, 24 × 19.2 cm), p. 94 (gelatin silver, 23.9 × 19.1 cm), by Lewis W. Hine, 1930–31, courtesy of the J. Paul Getty Museum, Los Angeles, California.